THE
CLASSICAL
MUSIC
FAKEBOOK

HAL•LEONARD®

Exclusive Distributors:
Hal Leonard, 7777 West Bluemound Road, Milwaukee, WI 53213 Email: info@halleonard.com
Hal Leonard Europe Limited, 42 Wigmore Street, Marylebone, London WIU 2 RY
Email: info@halleonardeurope.com
Hal Leonard Australia Pty. Ltd., 4 Lentara Court, Cheltenham, Victoria 9132, Australia
Email: info@halleonard.com.au
Order No. AM92350 ISBN 0-7119-4426-1 This book © Copyright 1995 by Hal Leonard

Compiled by Peter Evans & Peter Lavender. Book design by Pearce Marchbank. Quarked by Ben May.
Printed in the United Kingdom

www.halleonard.com

Symphony No.40 In G Minor
1st Movement Theme

Composed by Wolfgang Amadeus Mozart

ADAGIO

Composed by Tommaso Albinoni

© Copyright 1995 Dorsey Brothers Music Limited, 8/9 Frith Street, London W1.
All Rights Reserved. International Copyright Secured.

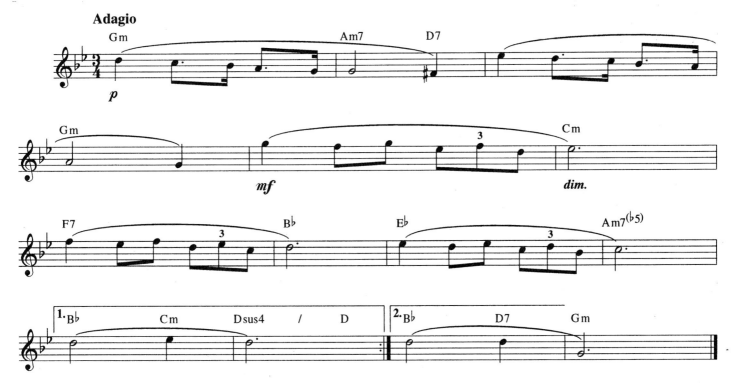

SYMPHONY No.3 In Eb (EROICA)
1ST MOVEMENT THEME

Composed by Ludwig van Beethoven

Hornpipe from Water Music

Composed by George Frideric Handel

SYMPHONY NO.6 (PASTORAL)
3RD MOVEMENT THEME

Composed by Ludwig van Beethoven

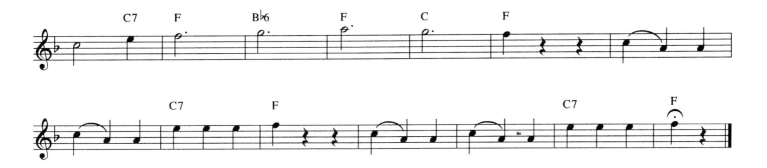

Polovtsian Dance from Prince Igor

Composed by Alexander Borodin

Il Bacio

Composed by Luigi Arditi

Symphony No. 1 In C Minor
4th Movement Theme

Composed by Johannes Brahms

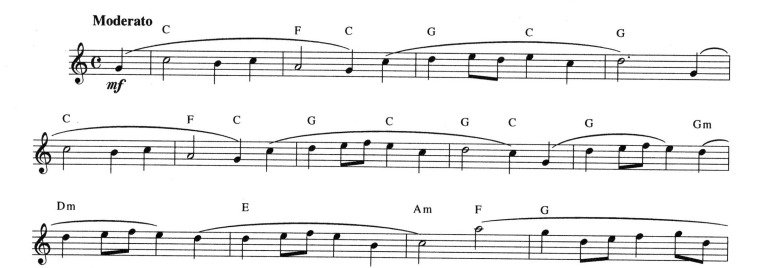

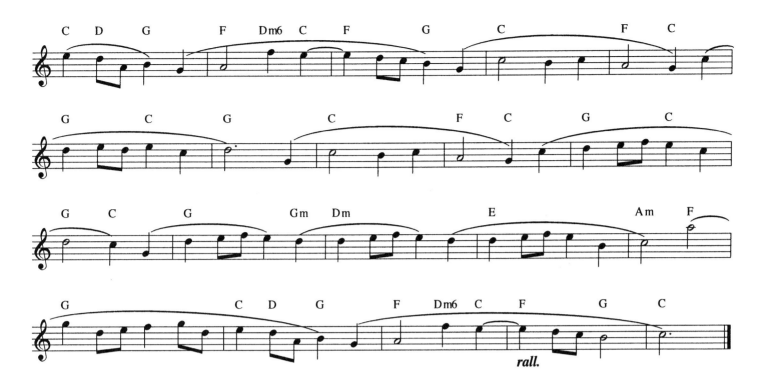

HUNGARIAN DANCE No.6

Composed by Johannes Brahms

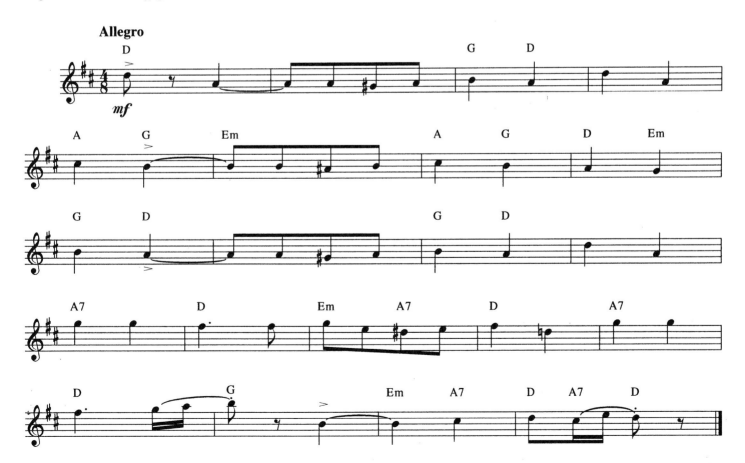

Variations On A Theme By Haydn
(St. Anthony Chorale)

Composed by Johannes Brahms

AIR ON THE G STRING

Composed by Johann Sebastian Bach

CLAIR DE LUNE

Composed by Claude Debussy

Andante

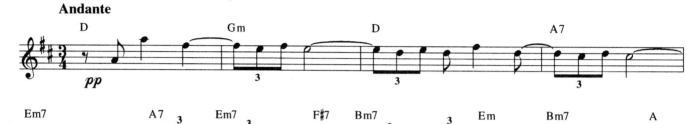

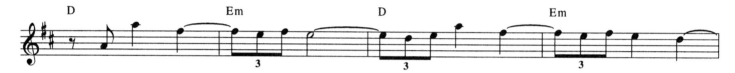

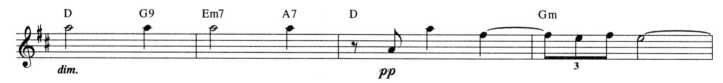

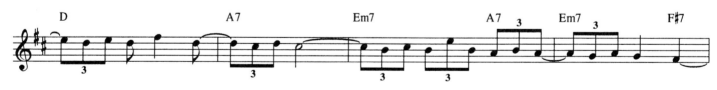

Rêverie

Composed by Claude Debussy

Minute Waltz

Composed by Frédéric Chopin

Symphony No.3 In F
3rd Movement Theme

Composed by Johannes Brahms

Moderato

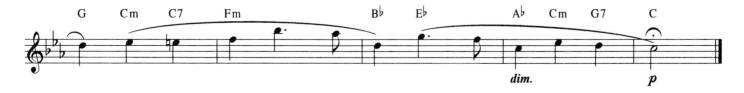

Adagio from Sonata No.8 In C Minor - (Pathétique)
2nd Movement Theme

Composed by Ludwig van Beethoven

Trumpet Voluntary

Composed by Jeremiah Clarke

Waltz Op.39 No.15

Composed by Johannes Brahms

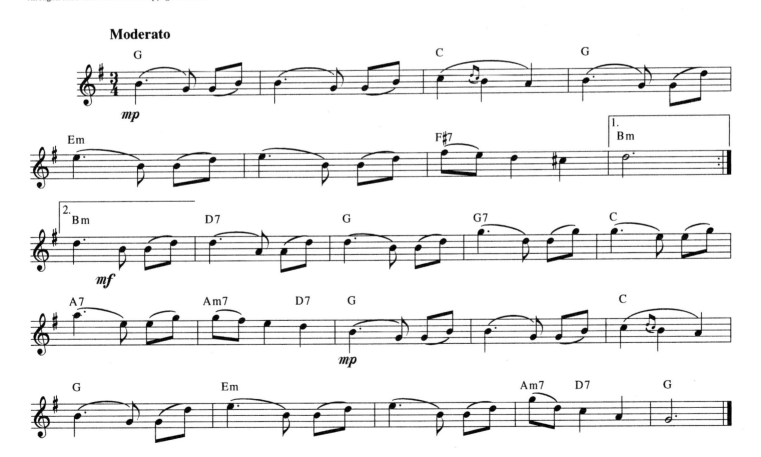

Hungarian Dance No.5

Composed by Johannes Brahms

Allegro moderato

Etude No.3

Composed by Frédéric Chopin

Toreador's Song from Carmen

Composed by Georges Bizet

Moderato

Songs My Mother Taught Me

Composed by Antonin Dvořák

Moderato

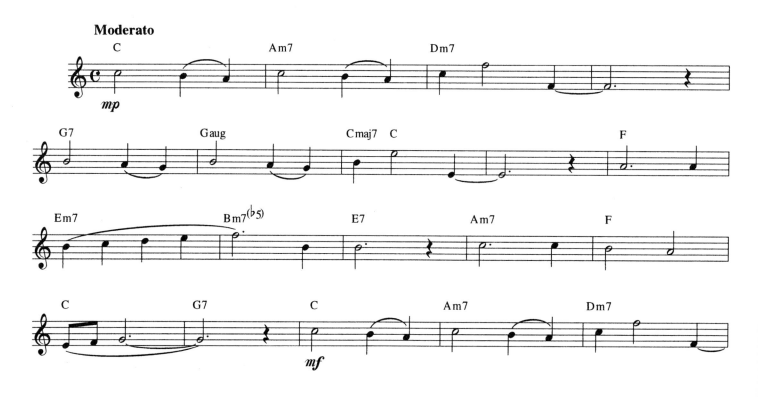

22

POEM

Composed by Zdeněk Fibich

MINUET IN G MAJOR

Composed by Johann Sebastian Bach

MARCH FROM ALCESTE

Composed by Christoph Willibald Gluck

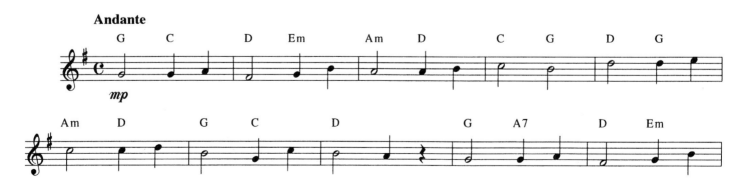

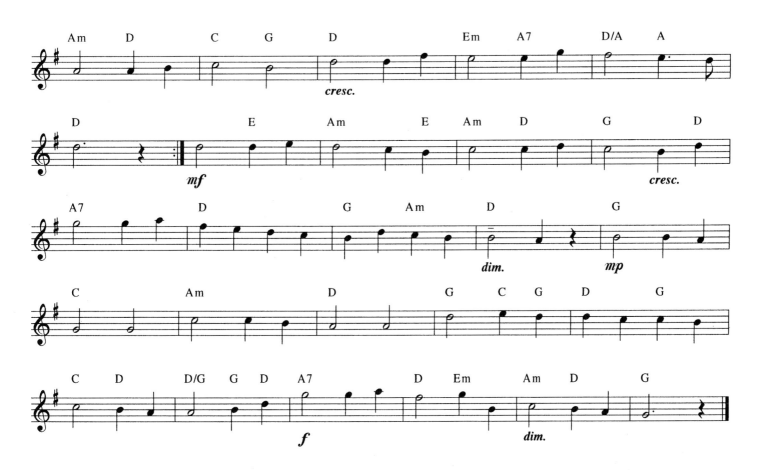

TRUMPET TUNE

Composed by Jeremiah Clarke

NOCTURNE FROM STRING QUARTET NO.2

Composed by Alexander Borodin

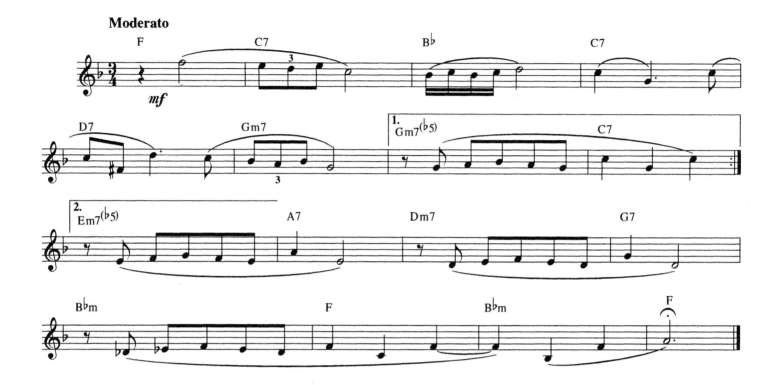

AVE MARIA

Composed by Charles Gounod

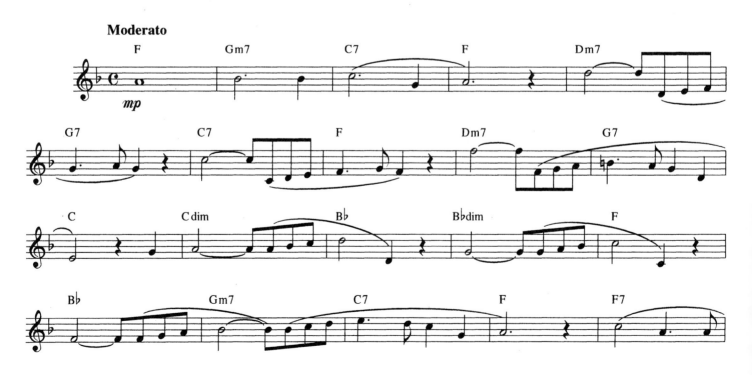

Ah! So Pure

Composed by Felix Von Flotow

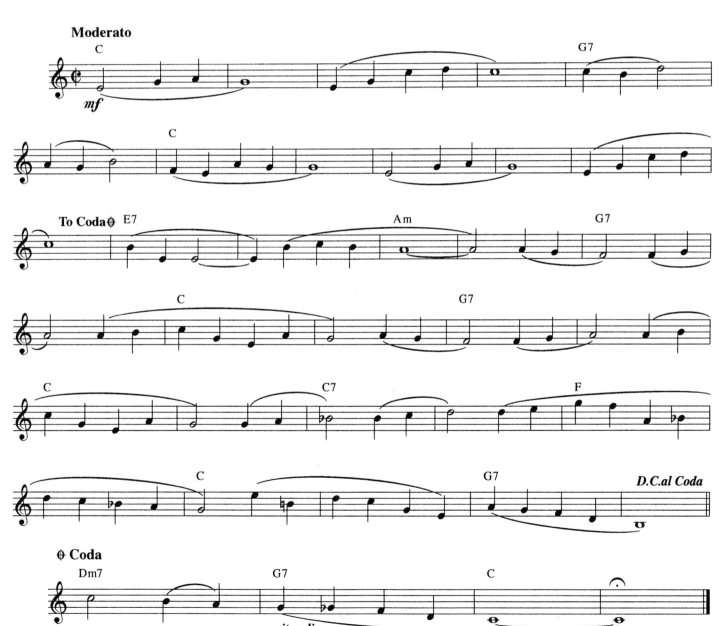

MORNING FROM PEER GYNT SUITE NO. 1

Composed by Edvard Grieg

MEDITATION FROM THAIS

Composed by Jules Massenet

Hallelujah Chorus from Messiah

Composed by George Frideric Handel

Symphony No.3 (Scottish)
3rd Movement Theme

Composed by Felix Mendelssohn-Bartholdy

I Know That My Redeemer Liveth from Messiah

Composed by George Frideric Handel

SYMPHONY NO.97 IN C
2ND MOVEMENT THEME

Composed by Franz Joseph Haydn

LARGO

Composed by George Frideric Handel

Sonata In C Minor
Last Movement Theme

Composed by Wolfgang Amadeus Mozart

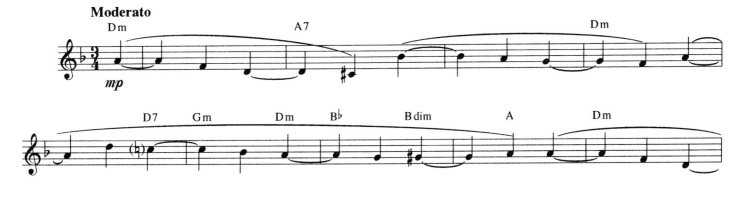

Espańa

Composed by Emmanuel Chabrier

Valse Lente from Coppélia

Composed by Léo Delibes

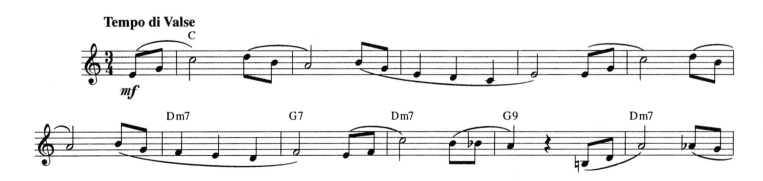

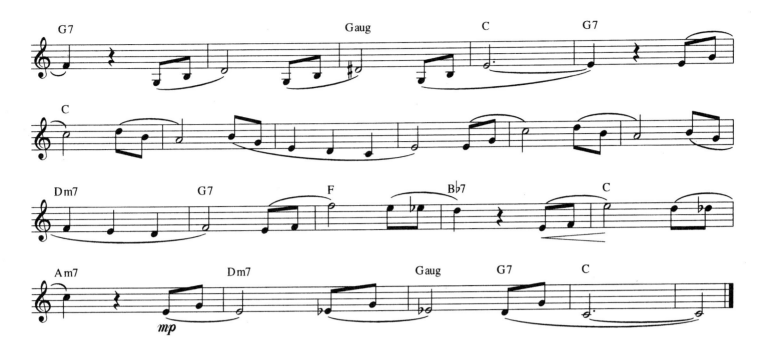

Serenade from Millions D'arlequin

Composed by Riccardo Drigo

LULLABY

Composed by Johannes Brahms

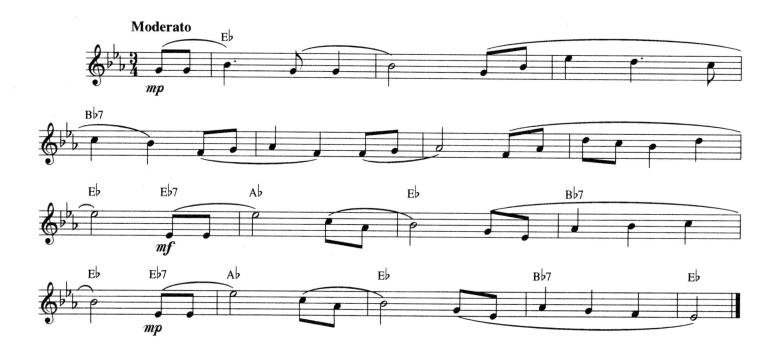

BERCEUSE FROM DOLLY SUITE

Composed by Gabriel Fauré

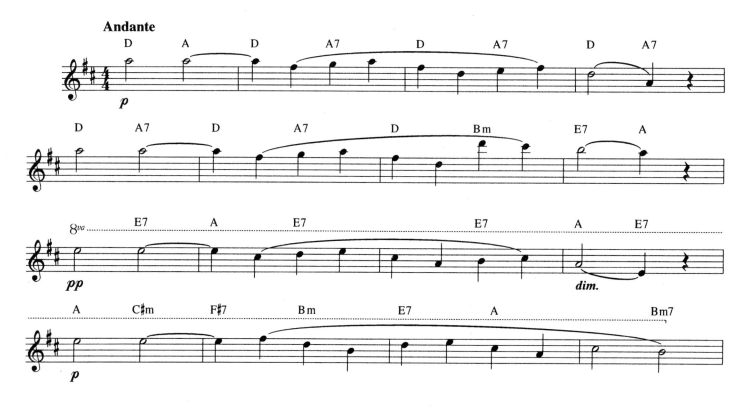

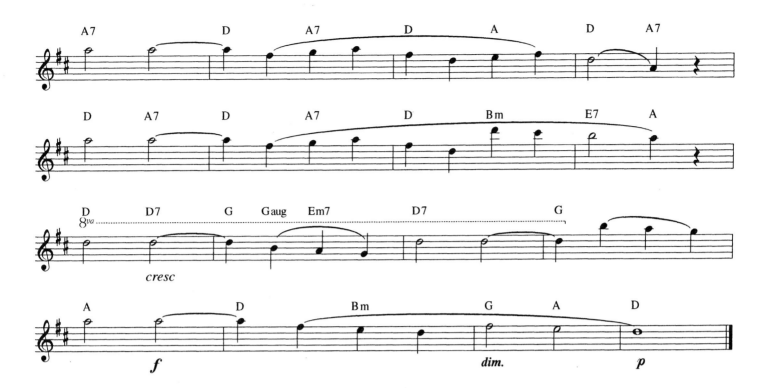

Nimrod from Enigma Variations

Composed by Sir Edward Elgar

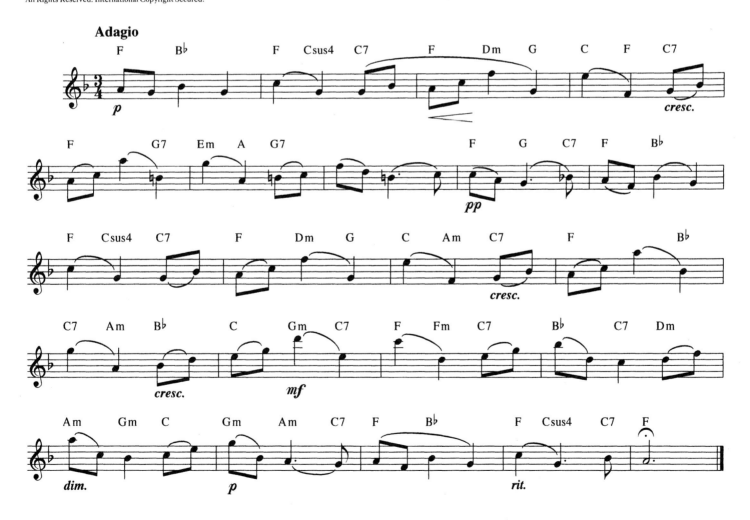

SYMPHONY NO. 104 IN D (LONDON)
2ND MOVEMENT THEME

Composed by Franz Joseph Haydn

MARCH FROM SCIPIONE

Composed by George Frideric Handel

SYMPHONY NO.9 (ODE TO JOY)-THEME

Composed by Ludwig van Beethoven

ON WINGS OF SONG

Composed by Felix Mendelssohn-Bartholdy

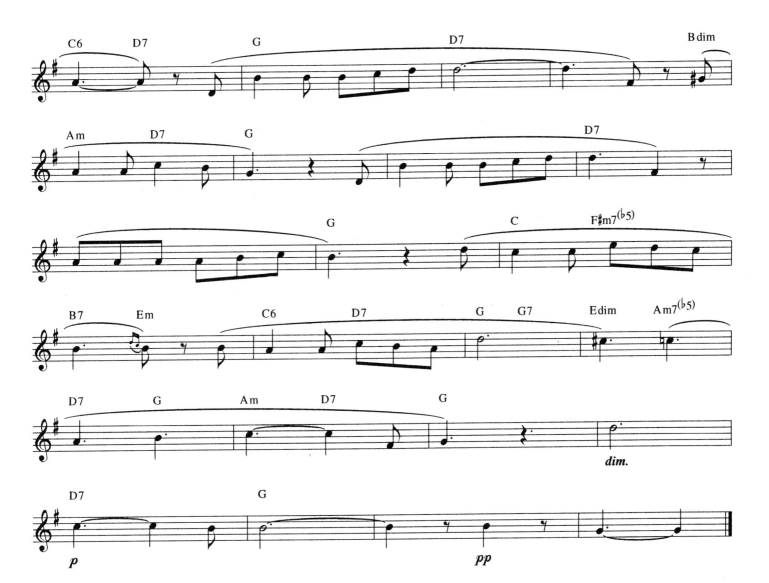

Prelude Op.28 No.7

Composed by Frédéric Chopin

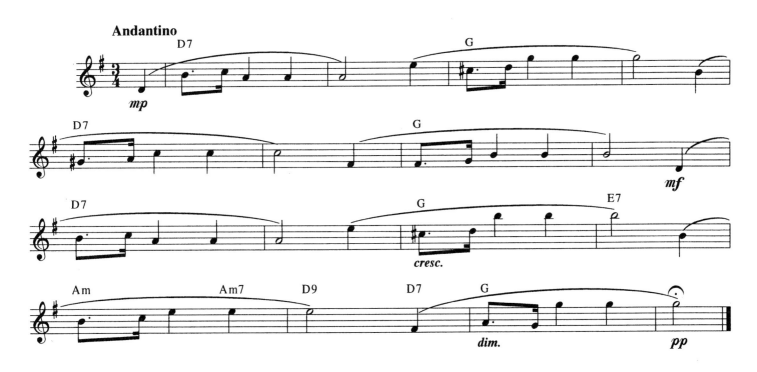

HUMORESKE

Composed by Antonin Dvořák

LIEBESTRAUM

Composed by Franz Liszt

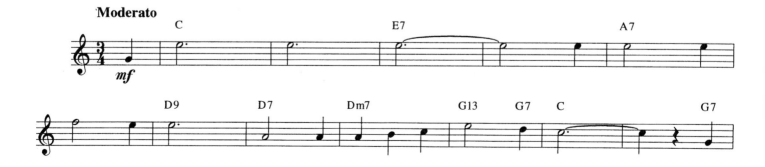

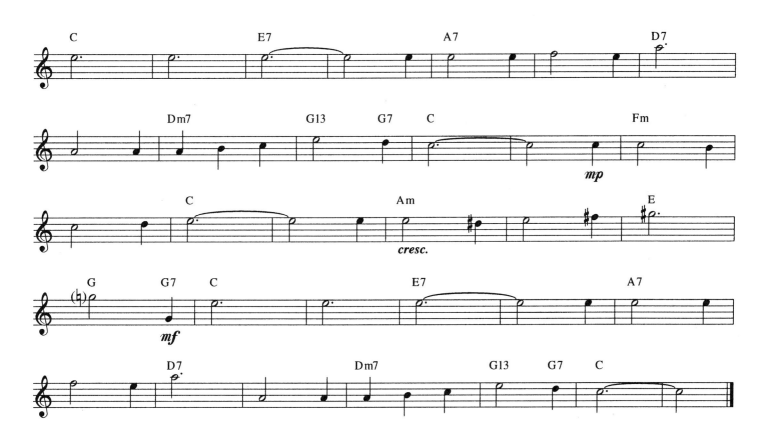

POMP AND CIRCUMSTANCE MARCH NO. 1

Composed by Sir Edward Elgar

Say Goodbye Now To Pastime
from The Marriage Of Figaro

Composed by Wolfgang Amadeus Mozart

Melody In F

Composed by Anton Rubinstein

AVE MARIA

Composed by Franz Schubert

Adagietto

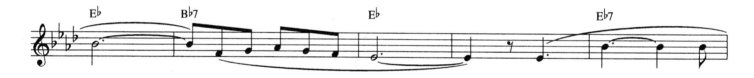

rit. e dim.

TELL ME FAIR LADIES
FROM THE MARRIAGE OF FIGARO

Composed by Wolfgang Amadeus Mozart

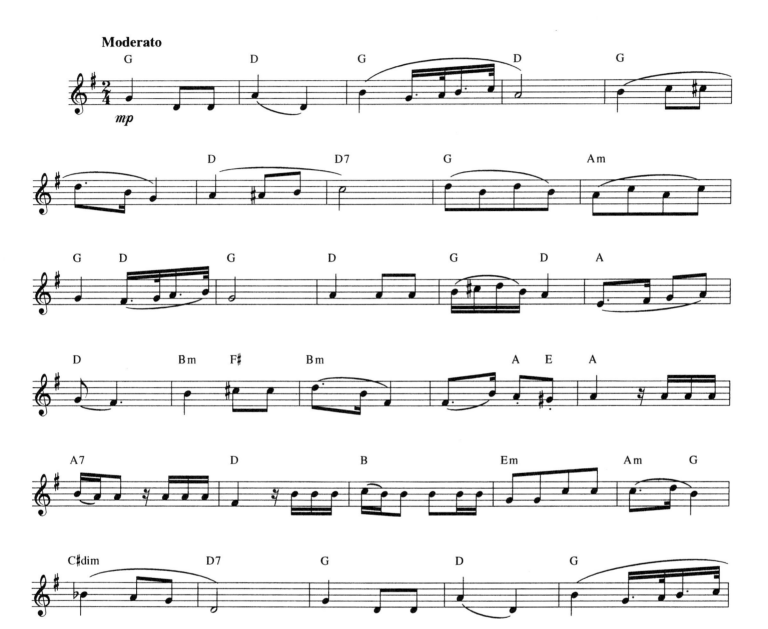

EMPEROR WALTZ

Composed by Johann Strauss II

Tempo di valse

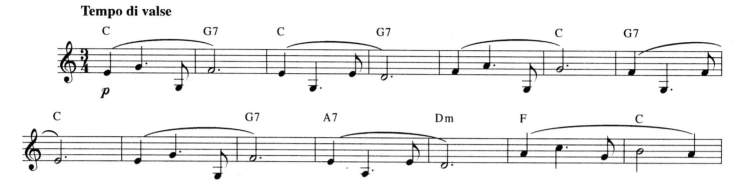

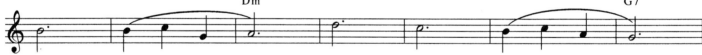

50

RONDO ALLA TURCA

Composed by Wolfgang Amadeus Mozart

Largo - From The New World Symphony
2nd Movement Theme

Composed by Antonin Dvořák

Hungarian March

Composed by Hector Berlioz

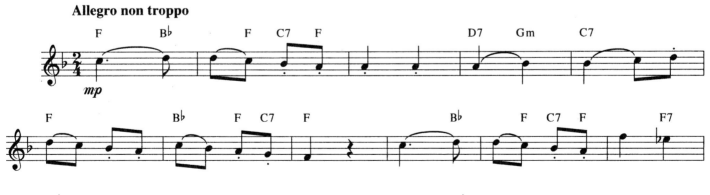

ALLELUIA FROM EXULTATE JUBILATE

Composed by Wolfgang Amadeus Mozart

SYMPHONY NO.4 (ITALIAN)
3RD MOVEMENT THEME

Composed by Felix Mendelssohn-Bartholdy

HUNGARIAN DANCE NO.4

Composed by Johannes Brahms

Tresor Waltz

Composed by Johann Strauss II

MARCH OF THE PRIESTS
FROM THE MAGIC FLUTE

Composed by Wolfgang Amadeus Mozart

PAVANE

Composed by Gabriel Fauré

AIR FROM WATER MUSIC

Composed by George Frideric Handel

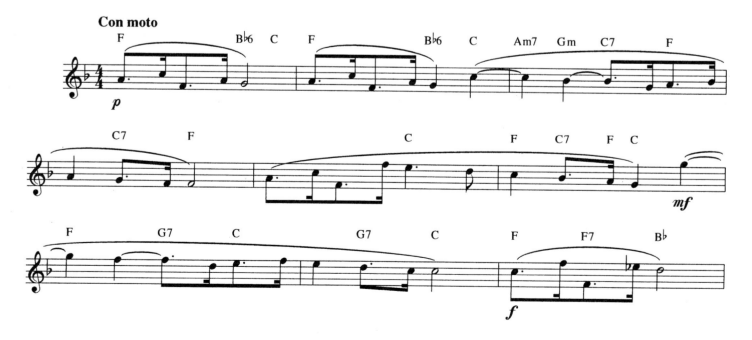

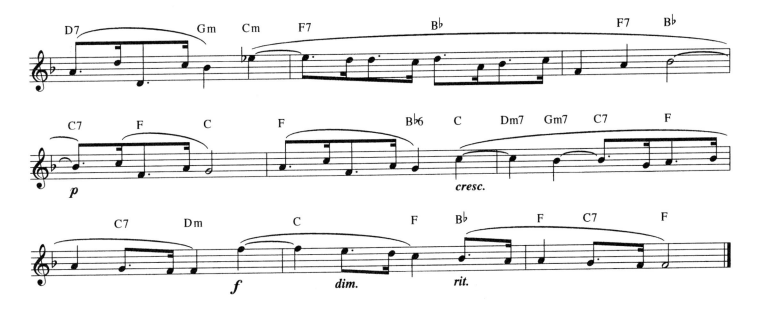

SEE THE CONQUERING HERO COMES FROM JUDAS MACCABAEUS

Composed by George Frideric Handel

MINUET NO. 2
FROM MUSIC FOR THE ROYAL FIREWORKS

Composed by George Frideric Handel

FANTAISIE IMPROMPTU OP.66 THEME

Composed by Frédéric Chopin

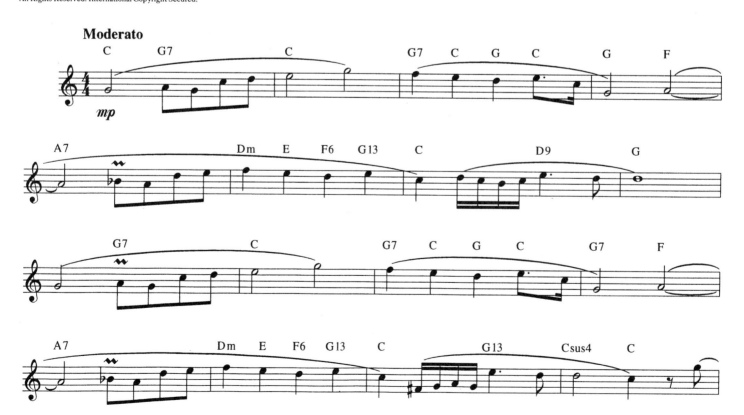

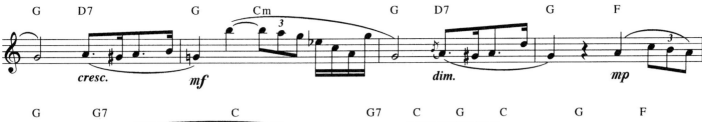

THEME FROM BALLADE OP.23

Composed by Frédéric Chopin

Minuetto
from Eine Kleine Nachtmusik

Composed by Wolfgang Amadeus Mozart

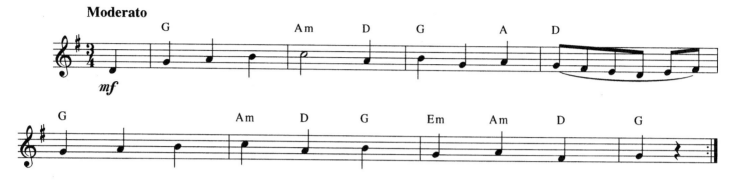

ROMANCE

Composed by Anton Rubinstein

NOCTURNE OP.55 NO.1

Composed by Frédéric Chopin

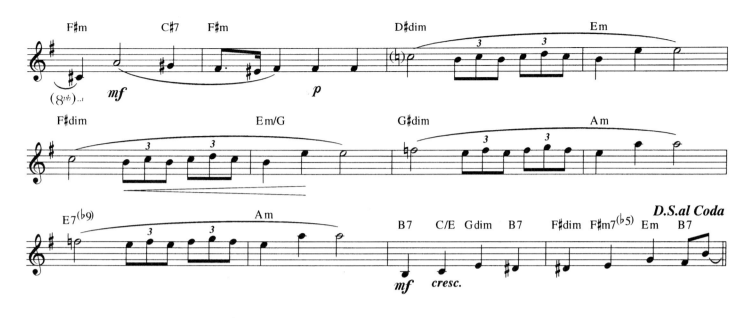

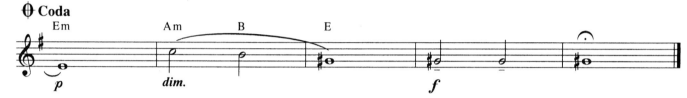

GYPSY LOVE SONG

Composed by Victor Herbert

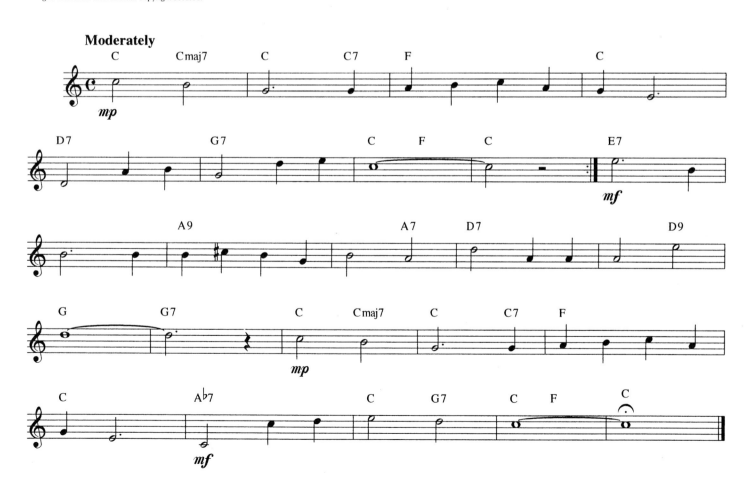

Nocturne Op.15 No.3

Composed by Frédéric Chopin

Là Ci Darem La Mano (You'll Lay Your Hand In Mine)
from Don Giovanni

Composed by Wolfgang Amadeus Mozart

Moderato

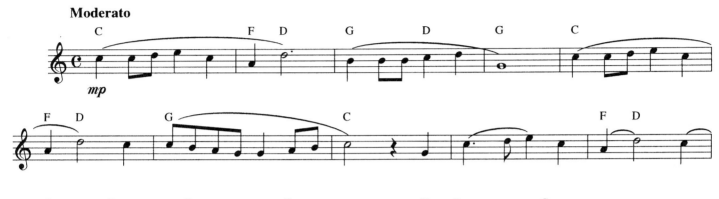

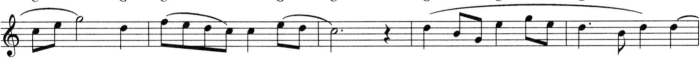

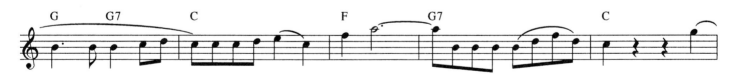

PRELUDE OP.28 NO.20

Composed by Frédéric Chopin

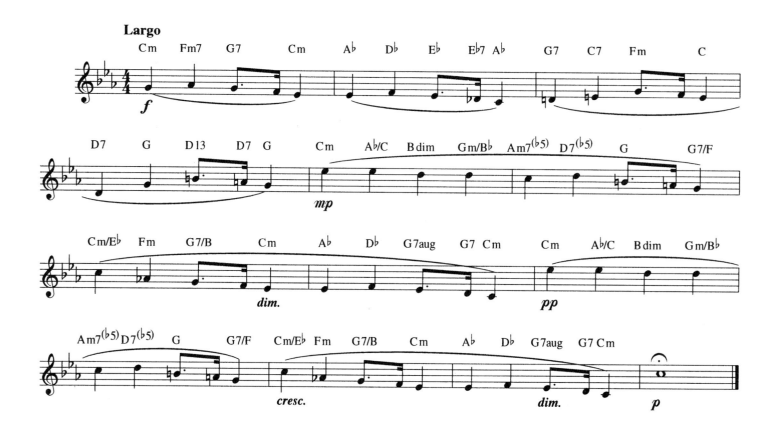

JUPITER FROM THE PLANETS SUITE

Composed by Gustav Holst

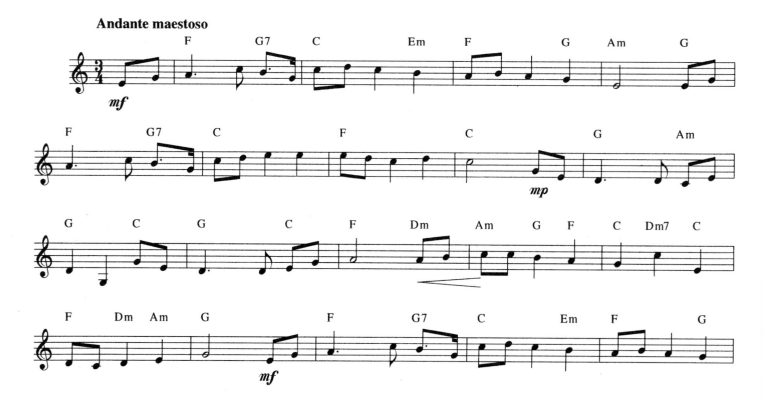

Minuetto Theme from Haffner Symphony

Composed by Wolfgang Amadeus Mozart

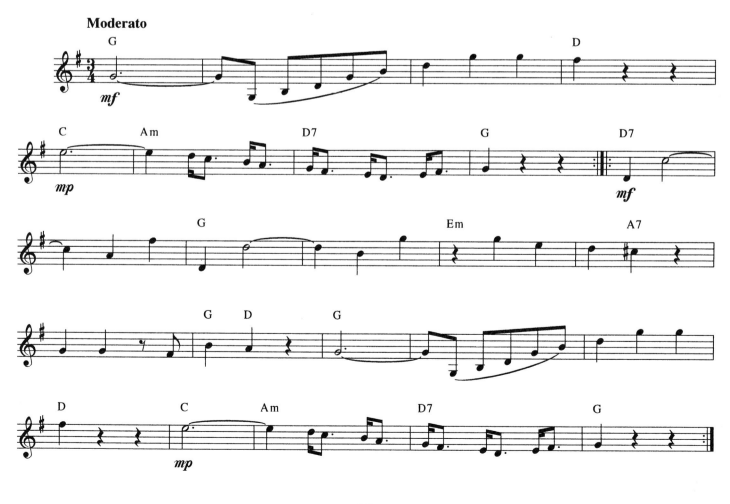

Tales From The Vienna Woods

Composed by Johann Strauss II

Tempo di valse

LOVE THEME FROM PAGLIACCI

Composed by Ruggiero Leoncavallo

MORNING PAPERS

Composed by Johann Strauss II

The Swan from Carnival Of The Animals

Composed by Camille Saint-Saëns

Vienna Blood

Composed by Johann Strauss II

O Isis And Osiris from The Magic Flute

Composed by Wolfgang Amadeus Mozart

To Friendship

Composed by Wolfgang Amadeus Mozart

Mazurka Op.33 No.2

Composed by Frédéric Chopin

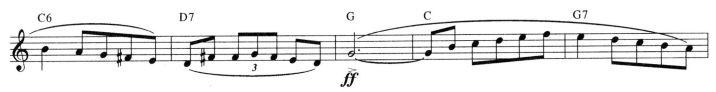

SYMPHONY NO.94 IN G (SURPRISE)
2ND MOVEMENT THEME

Composed by Franz Joseph Haydn

Waves Of The Danube

Composed by Iosif Ivanovici

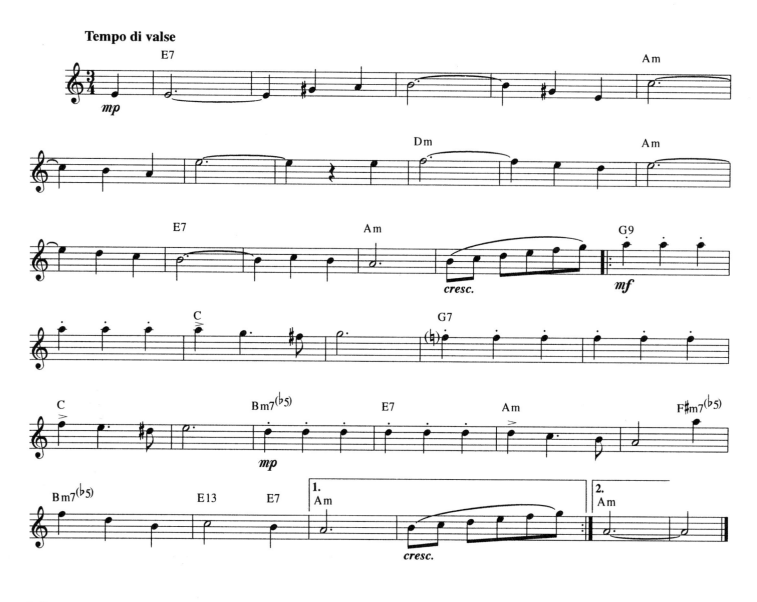

Nocturne
from A Midsummer Night's Dream

Composed by Felix Mendelssohn-Bartholdy

SARABANDE FROM SUITE XI

Composed by George Frideric Handel

Andante

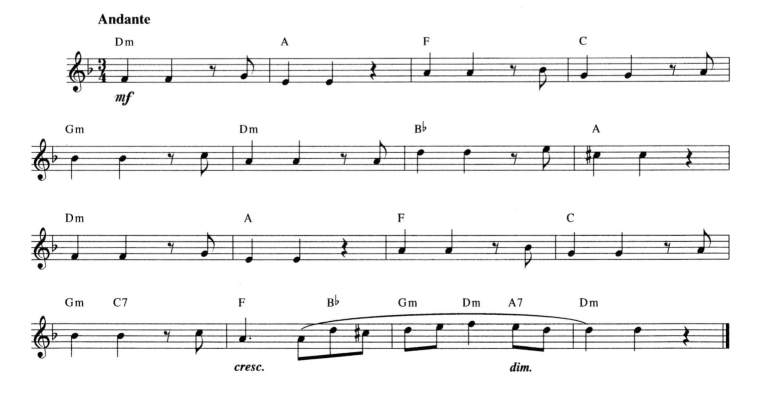

TRITSCH TRATSCH POLKA

Composed by Johann Strauss II

Allegretto

Pilgrims' Chorus from Tannhäuser

Composed by Richard Wagner

WALTZ FROM FAUST

Composed by Charles Gounod

Nocturne Op.9 No.2

Composed by Frédéric Chopin

Piano Concerto In B♭ - Slow Movement

Composed by Wolfgang Amadeus Mozart

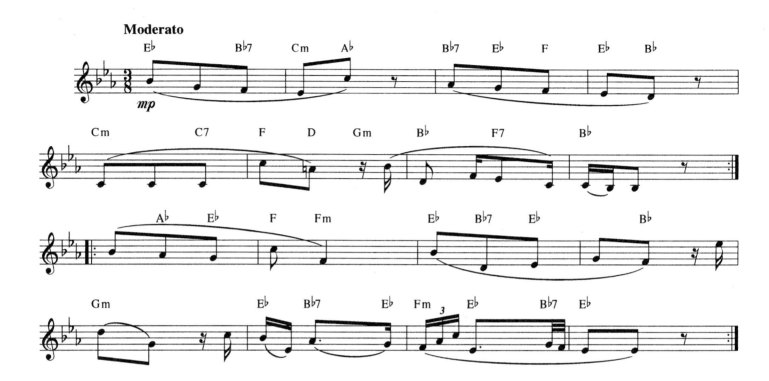

Skaters' Waltz

Composed by Emile Waldteufel

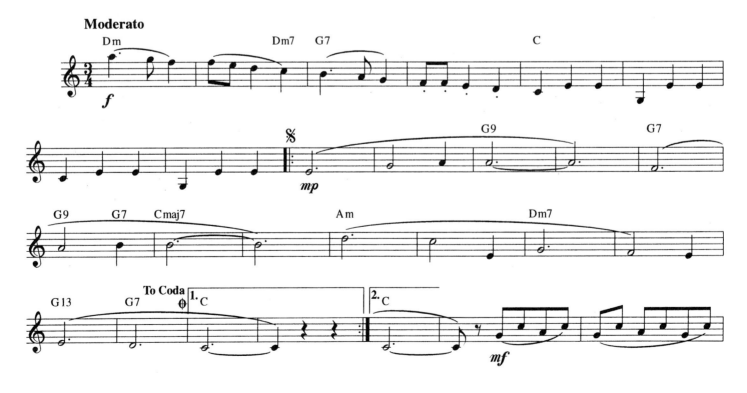

MENUET A L'ANTIQUE - THEME OP. 14 No. 1

Composed by Ignacy Paderewski

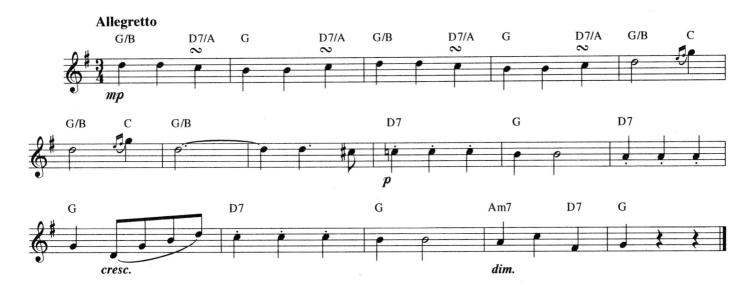

The Harmonious Blacksmith

Composed by George Frideric Handel

Anitra's Dance
from Peer Gynt Suite No. 1

Composed by Edvard Grieg

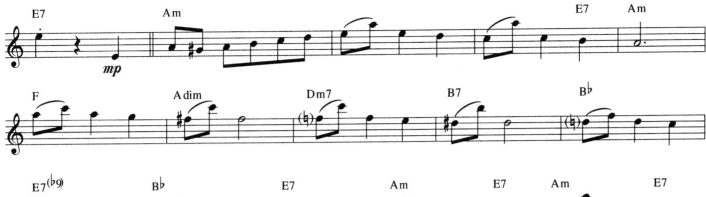

Symphony No.6 (Pathétique)
1st Movement Theme

Composed by Peter Ilyich Tchaikovsky

WEDDING MARCH
FROM A MIDSUMMER NIGHT'S DREAM

Composed by Felix Mendelssohn-Bartholdy

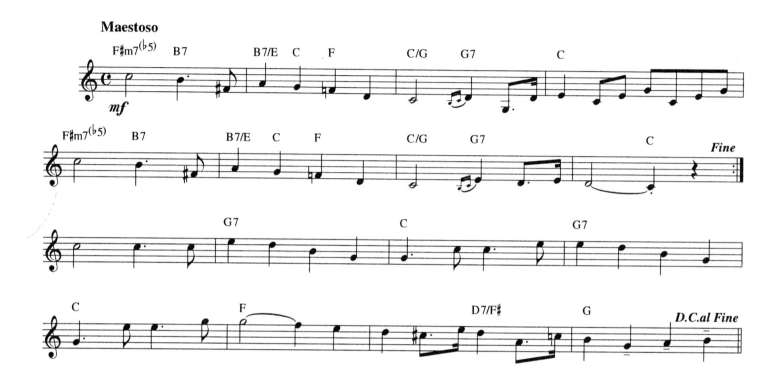

MINUET FROM SONATA IN E♭

Composed by Wolfgang Amadeus Mozart

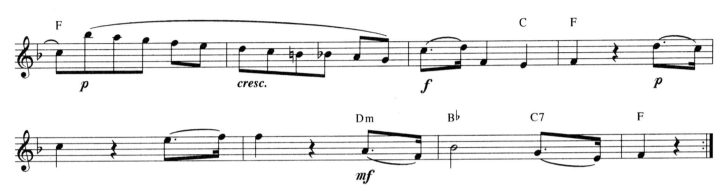

La Donna E Mobile from Rigoletto

Composed by Giuseppe Verdi

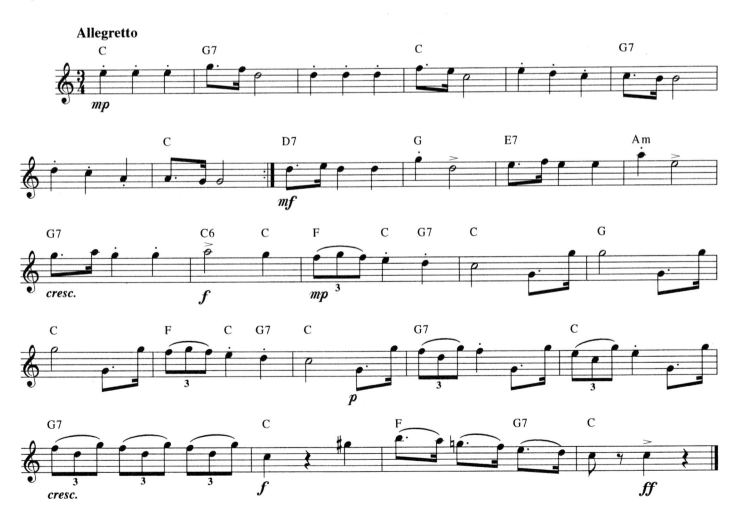

O My Beloved Father from Gianni Schicchi

Composed by Giacomo Puccini

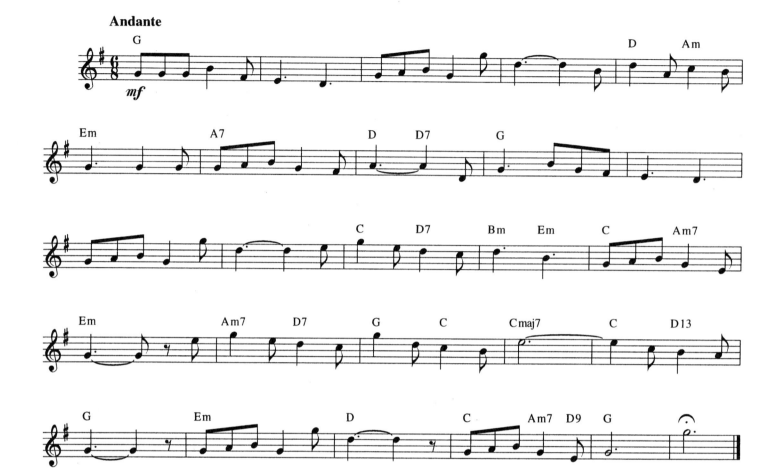

Eine Kleine Nachtmusik 1st Movement Theme

Composed by Wolfgang Amadeus Mozart

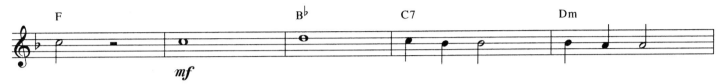

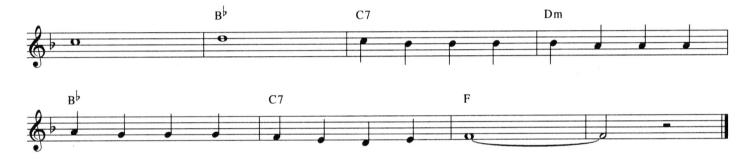

CAPRICE

Composed by Niccolo Paganini

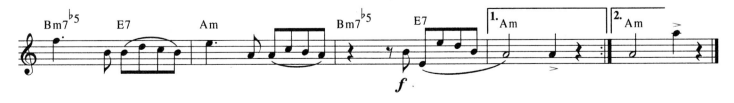

ROMANCE FROM THE PEARL FISHERS

Composed by Georges Bizet

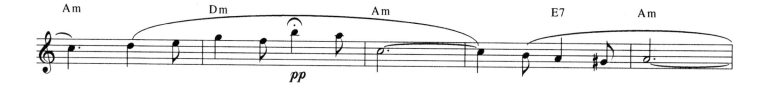

MUSETTA'S WALTZ FROM LA BOHÈME

Composed by Giacomo Puccini

Mattinata

Composed by Ruggiero Leoncavallo

Autumn from The Four Seasons

Composed by Antonio Vivaldi

94

Clarinet Concerto Theme

Composed by Wolfgang Amadeus Mozart

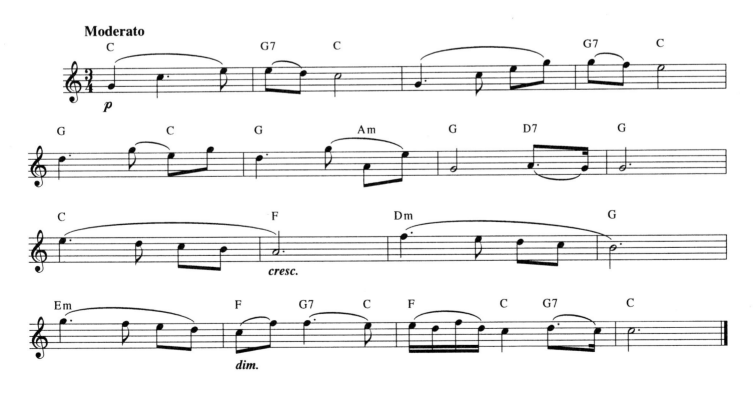

Die Fledermaus Waltz

Composed by Johann Strauss II

Minuet In F

Composed by Wolfgang Amadeus Mozart

Sonata No. 15
1st Movement Theme

Composed by Wolfgang Amadeus Mozart

My Heart At Thy Sweet Voice

Composed by Camille Saint-Saëns

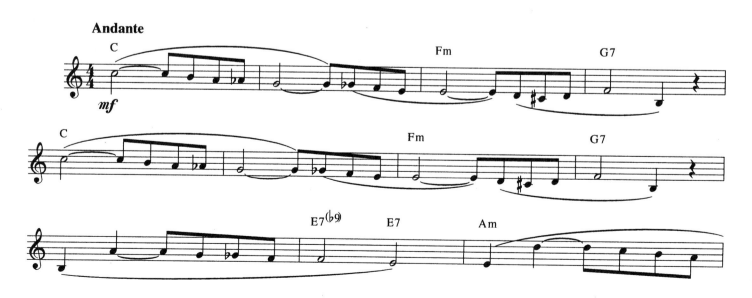

Plaisir D'amour

Composed by Giovanni Paolo Martini

SYMPHONY NO.6 (PATHÉTIQUE)
MARCH THEME

Composed by Peter Ilyich Tchaikovsky

SHEHERAZADE

Composed by Nikolai Rimsky-Korsakov

Violin Sonata In E♭
Last Movement Theme

Composed by Wolfgang Amadeus Mozart

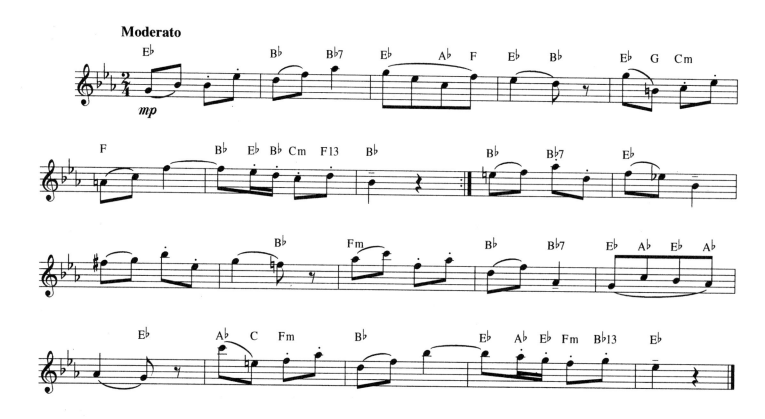

Waltz Op. 34 No. 1

Composed by Frédéric Chopin

Piano Concerto No. 1
1st Movement Theme

Composed by Peter Ilyich Tchaikovsky

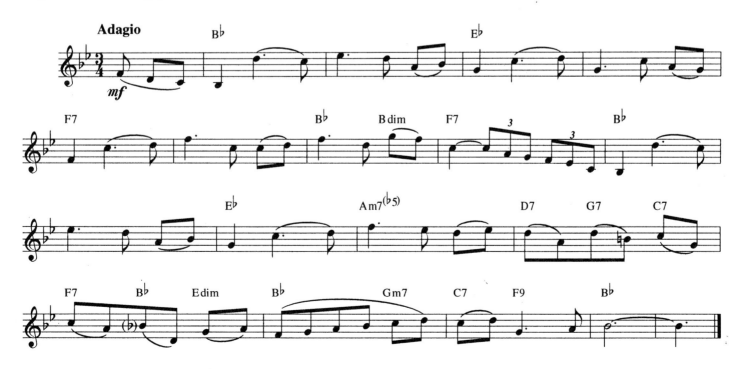

Sleeping Beauty Waltz

Composed by Peter Ilyich Tchaikovsky

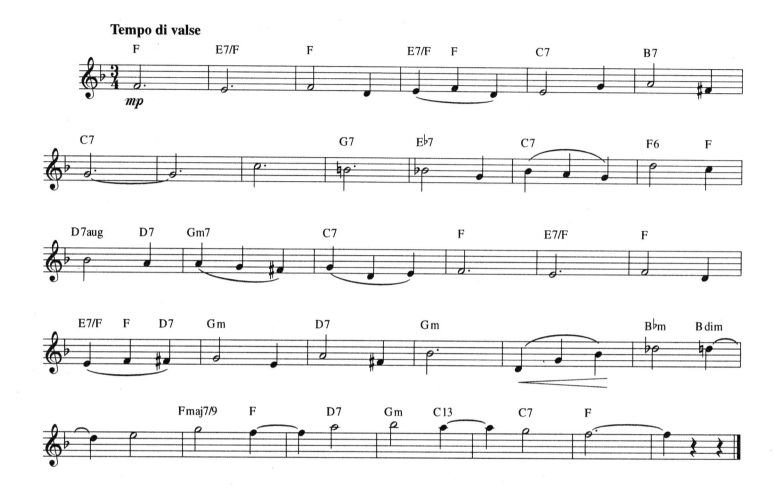

Serenata

Composed by Enrico Toselli

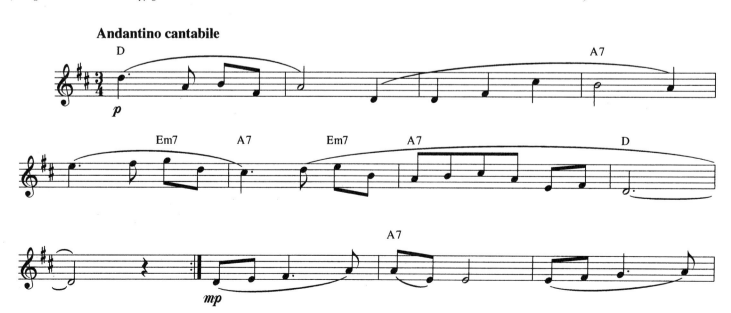

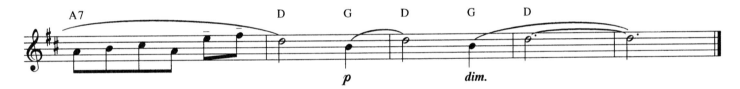

Anvil Chorus from Il Trovatore

Composed by Giuseppe Verdi

Piano Concerto No.21
2nd Movement Theme

Composed by Wolfgang Amadeus Mozart

Waltz Op.69 No.1

Composed by Frédéric Chopin

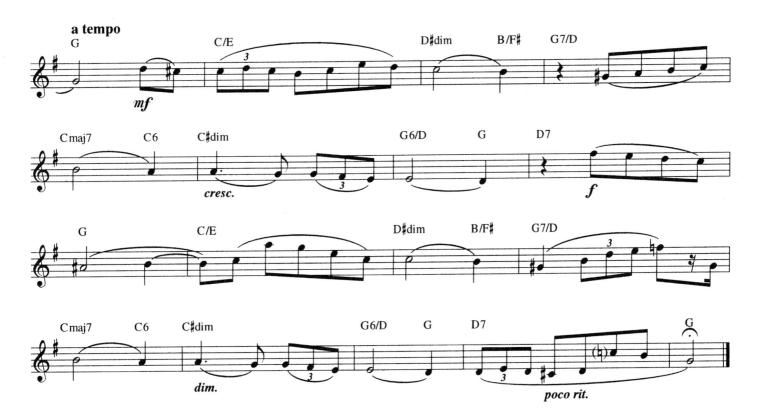

Sailors' Dance from Dido And Aeneas

Composed by Henry Purcell

Minuet from Berenice

Composed by George Frideric Handel

SYMPHONY No.6 (PATHÉTIQUE)
2ND MOVEMENT THEME

Composed by Peter Ilyich Tchaikovsky

Grazioso

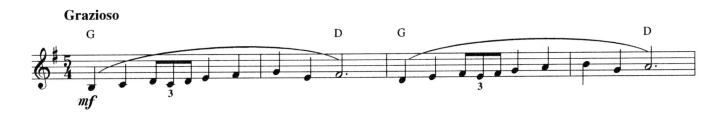

Unfinished Symphony
1st Movement Theme

Composed by Franz Schubert

Allegro moderato

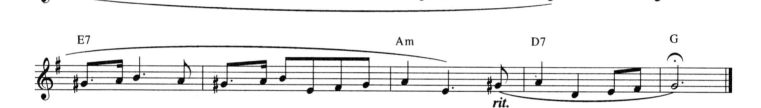

Symphony No.50 In D
2nd Movement Theme

Composed by Wolfgang Amadeus Mozart

Moderato

WILLIAM TELL OVERTURE-THEME

Composed by Gioacchino Rossini

Kaiser Waltz

Composed by Johann Strauss II

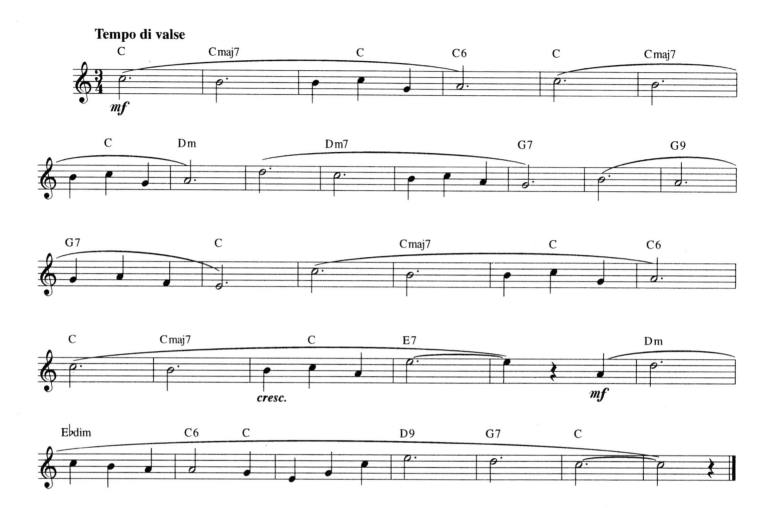

Bridal Chorus from Lohengrin

Composed by Richard Wagner

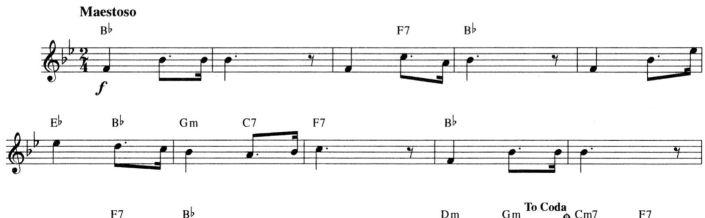

DANCE OF THE HOURS

Composed by Amilcare Ponchielli

The Happy Farmer

Composed by Robert Schumann

Romeo And Juliet (Theme)

Composed by Peter Ilyich Tchaikovsky

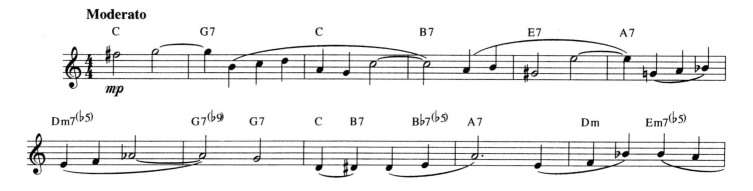

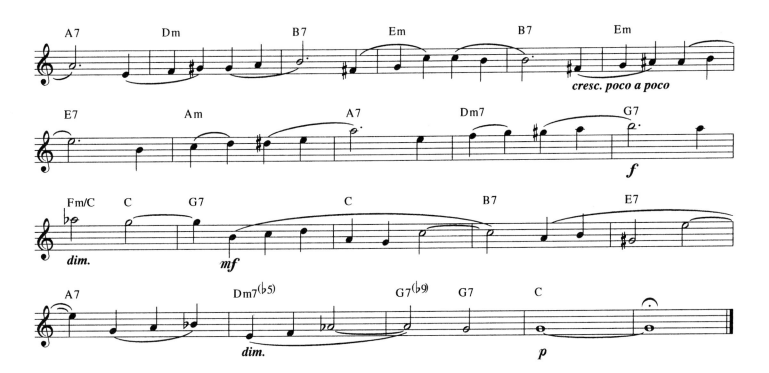

Capriccio Italienne

Composed by Peter Ilyich Tchaikovsky

SYMPHONY NO.5
2ND MOVEMENT THEME

Composed by Peter Ilyich Tchaikovsky

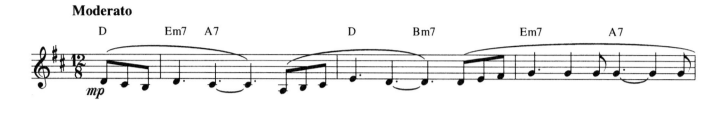

SYMPHONY NO.5 IN B♭
2ND MOVEMENT THEME

Composed by Franz Schubert

VILLAGE SWALLOWS

Composed by Josef Strauss

RONDEAU FROM ABDELAZER

Composed by Henry Purcell

THE HUNTSMEN'S CHORUS

Composed by Carl Maria Von Weber

Rêve de Printemps

Composed by Johann Strauss II

Waltz from Swan Lake

Composed by Peter Ilyich Tchaikovsky

Trout Quintet
4th Movement Theme

Composed by Franz Schubert

WALTZ OF THE FLOWERS
FROM THE NUTCRACKER SUITE

Composed by Peter Ilyich Tchaikovsky

Tempo di valse

ROMANCE FROM EINE KLEINE NACHTMUSIK

Composed by Wolfgang Amadeus Mozart

BLUE DANUBE WALTZ

Composed by Johann Strauss II

124

The Manly Heart That Claims Our Duty from The Magic Flute

Composed by Wolfgang Amadeus Mozart

© Copyright 1995 Dorsey Brothers Music Limited, 8/9 Frith Street, London W1.
All Rights Reserved. International Copyright Secured.

SYMPHONY NO.4 (ITALIAN)
2ND MOVEMENT THEME

Composed by Felix Mendelssohn-Bartholdy

RONDO THEME
FROM VIOLIN CONCERTO IN D MAJOR

Composed by Wolfgang Amadeus Mozart

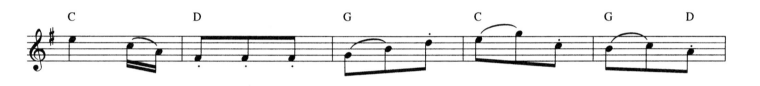

SPHÄREN-KLÄNGE WALTZ

Composed by Josef Strauss

Tempo di valse